design ART DECO quilts

MIX & MATCH SIMPLE GEOMETRIC SHAPES

DON LINN

C&T PUBLISHING

Text copyright © 2010 by Don Linn

Artwork copyright © 2010 by C&T Publishing, Inc.

Publisher: Amy Marson

Creative Director: Gailen Runge

Acquisitions Editor: Susanne Woods

Editor: Liz Aneloski

Technical Editors: Ann Haley and Nanette S. Zeller

Copyeditor/Proofreader: Wordfirm Inc.

Cover/Book Designer: Kristen Yenche

Page Layout Artist: Peter Chamberlain

Production Coordinator: Zinnia Heinzmann

Production Editor: Alice Mace Nakanishi

Illustrator: Mary E. Flynn

Photography by Christina Carty-Francis and Diane Pedersen of C&T Publishing, Inc., unless otherwise noted.

Published by C&T Publishing, Inc., P.O. Box 1456, Lafayette, CA 94549

Library of Congress Cataloging-in-Publication Data

Linn, Don, 1945 Aug. 16–
  Design art deco quilts : mix & match simple geometric shapes / Don Linn.
    p. cm.
  ISBN 978-1-57120-851-4 (soft cover)
  1. Patchwork--Patterns. 2. Quilting--Patterns. I. Title.

TT835.L546 2010
746.46'041--dc22
                              2009020109

Printed in China

10 9 8 7 6 5 4 3 2 1

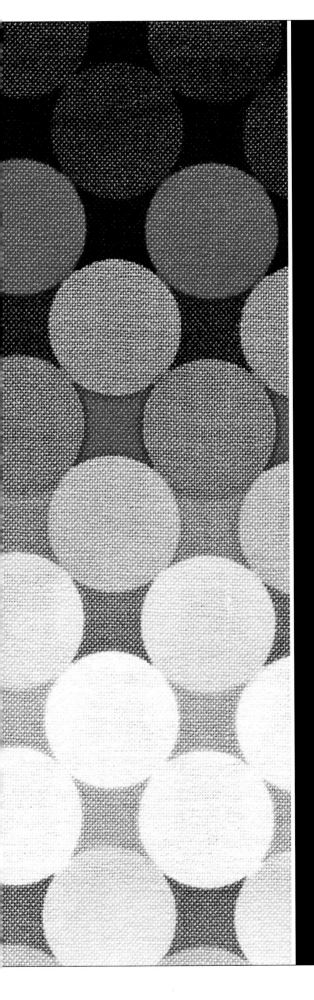

CONTENTS

Dedication

This book is dedicated to my loving wife, Donna.

Thank you for being so supportive and never doubting me, even when I doubted myself. Most of all, thank you for putting up with my insanity for all of these years.

You are the best.

Acknowledgments

I want to thank all of my Deco Dolls—Fran Brooks, Louise Wilson, Tenna Olsen, Kathy Fletcher, Merri Caywood, Deborah Storz, Sharon McDaniel, Connie Livingston, and Charlotte Uchimura—for critiquing this technique from start to finish. Special thanks for the wonderful quilts that you made and that are shown in this book. Without you this book would not have happened.

Thank you Liz Aneloski, my editor, for making me look so good.

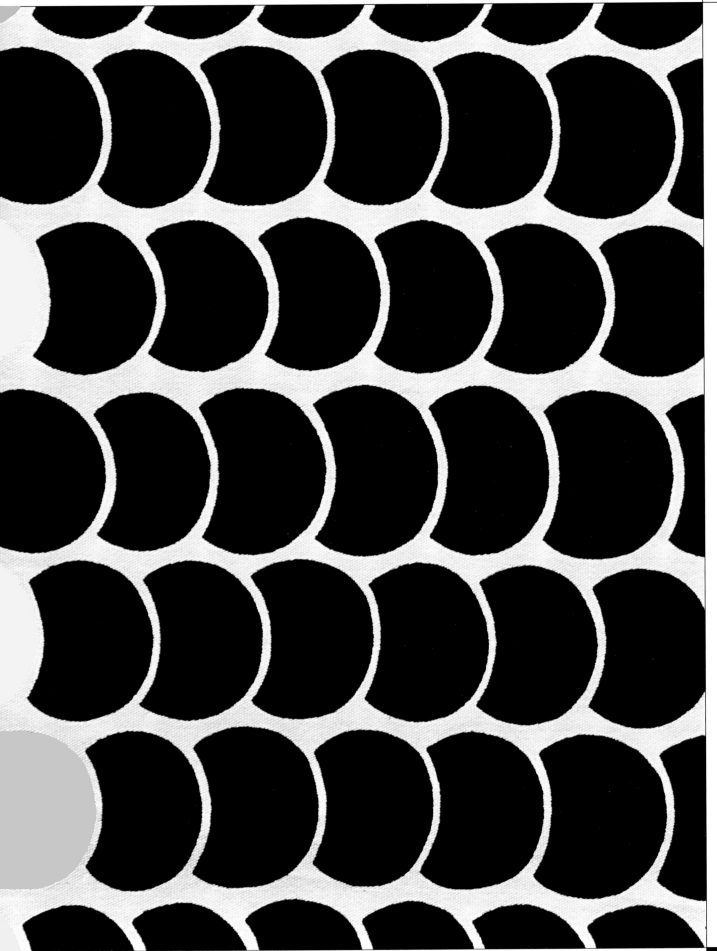

CHAPTER **1**

ART DECO DESIGN CONCEPTS

The style that is known as art deco came into being between the First and Second World Wars. It was first introduced in France in 1928 at the *Exposition Internationale des Arts Décoratifs et Industriels Modernes* (International Exposition of Modern Decorative and Industrial Arts). The term *art deco* was coined by Bevis Hillier, a student of this style, by shortening the title of the 1928 show. In 1969, Mr. Hillier titled his book *Art Deco*, which covered this style. This book, along with the 1971 Minneapolis Institute of Arts exhibition entitled *The World of Art Deco*, firmly cemented the name for this rather broad style.

As a child I remember the TV presence of Ethyl Merman as a guest on *The Ed Sullivan Show*. Some may remember her belting out the lyrics on the right from the old Cole Porter standard "Anything Goes."

This verse aptly describes the general attitude of most people during the twenties and thirties. During that time, between the two world wars, designers worked in two diverse schools of thought. One area of design was in the use of florals; nearly all of these designs were highly stylized or abstract in nature. The other school of thought concentrated on making designs clean and uncluttered as a way of divorcing themselves from the preceding art nouveau era.

Mass production was becoming commonplace during this time, and the designers affected all things imaginable. Many designs were very angular in nature instead of the traditional shapes of the past. Some referred to these designs as "machine arts."

In olden days a glimpse of stocking Was looked on as something shocking, But now, God knows, Anything goes.

—Cole Porter

Other designs attempted to capture the futuristic streamlined look of what was yet to come. Here you would see more flowing lines as the designers tried to capture the feeling of flowing motion in their work.

Architecture was not exempt from the art deco influence during this era. Some well-known examples are the Empire State Building, the Chrysler Building, and Rockefeller Center.

One area where the two schools of design seemed to come together was in movie theaters that were built during this time. I am fortunate enough to live in a city where we have one of these fine old theaters that has been restored to its original splendor. Here at the Cascade Theater in Redding, California, you can see examples of clean geometric designs and very elaborate floral designs being used together.

I first became interested in art deco designs when I was working with fused glass while taking a break from quilting. The simple geometric designs readily lent themselves to cutting and fusing glass.

It occurred to me that these simple geometric designs might lend themselves to some new and unusual quilt designs. That is what led to the inspiration for this book.

I hope you enjoy this design technique as much as I do and that you are encouraged to try something new and create your own works of art.

Art deco tea set

Fused glass platter by author

Art deco water pitcher

Interior of Cascade Theater

Art deco toaster

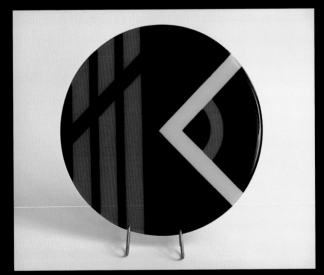
Fused glass disk by author

CHAPTER **2**

TOOLS, SUPPLIES, AND FABRIC SELECTION

You probably already have on hand most of the tools that you will need if you have made quilts in the past. Any other additional tools and supplies that you will need are readily available at office supply stores, at home building centers, or on the Internet. Some of the tools will be used for both designing and sewing. A few additional supplies are listed under Free-form Curves (page 58).

DESIGN TOOLS AND SUPPLIES

- Foamcore board (16″ × 20″ minimum)
- Graph paper, 8 squares per inch (11″ × 17″ sheets preferred, or 8½″ × 11″)
- Colored construction paper (package of multiple colors)
- Permanent marking pen
- Pencil
- Paper-cutting scissors
- 45° triangle (or ruler with a 45° line)
- Inexpensive drafting compass
- Beam compass or yardstick compass
- Glue pen or gluestick
- Straight pins (strong ones)
- Eraser

SEWING TOOLS

- Sewing machine
- ¼″ pressure foot
- Rotary cutter
- Quilter's ruler (24″ is a handy size)
- Cutting mat
- Straight pins
- Self-adhesive note pad (small)
- Seam ripper (just in case)
- Scissors (small, sharp pair)
- Stiletto

Sewing tools

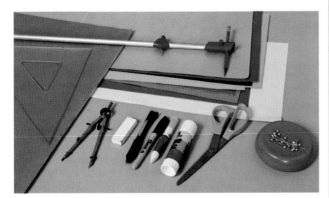

Design tools and supplies

FABRIC SELECTION

When choosing fabrics, keep in mind the previously mentioned Cole Porter song "Anything Goes" and you will be in good shape.

Seriously, I think that fabric selection is a very personal matter and should be dictated by your personal preferences. I know what fabrics I like and what I am comfortable working with, and I am sure you feel the same way about your choices. (That is not to say that we should not force ourselves to try new things.)

I tend to like big, bold prints that really jump out and get my attention. The desire to be able to use big pieces of these fabrics was one of the things that led me to start making my art deco quilts. I wanted a way to be able to use these beautiful prints without having to cut them up into small pieces and then sew them back together in what looks to me to be a jumbled mess.

In addition, I seem to gravitate to what I call strong colors and prints. I do not often use muted, earthy colors in my quilts. I think by looking at the quilts (see Gallery, pages 37–53) that I have made for this book, you will get a better understanding of my tastes.

In Chapter 4, I've provided two methods for calculating the amount of fabric you'll need for your project (see Estimating Yardage, page 36). These methods are applicable to the project quilt in the book or for a quilt design of your own. With that being said, I will give you a few thoughts on how I choose my fabrics.

Background Fabrics

Because of the design structure of these quilts, there will probably be some pretty big areas of background fabric. That means there will be quite a few seams in the open background areas because of the way the piecing sequence goes.

It bothers my eye to see a print with a close repeat cut up and sewn back together. To me this is very distracting, and I tend to spend too much time focusing on this hodgepodge of cut-up designs that make no sense. An example would be to have a piece of fabric with chickens on it. It would not look good to cut this up and then piece a block with a chicken's foot sticking out of its head. This may sound ridiculous, but I think you understand what I am talking about.

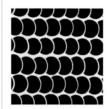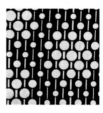

Hodgepodge prints

For the background, I recommend using fabrics that when cut up and sewn back together have no discernable disruption to the print. If the background appears to be uniform at first glance, your eye will not come to rest on it but will instead travel around the main design elements.

The choices for the background fall into four broad categories: solids, tone-on-tones, white-on-whites or some other shade, and small prints that appear to be random with no visible repeating pattern.

Solids

Solid fabrics can range in color from pure white to black and everything in between.

Solid-colored fabrics

Tone-on-Tones

Tone-on-tone fabrics, including some batiks, will have a repeating pattern, but the pattern is usually so soft and subtle that it is virtually impossible to pick out. If you are in doubt, you can always go with one of these fabrics and be confident that you will have a successful background to your design.

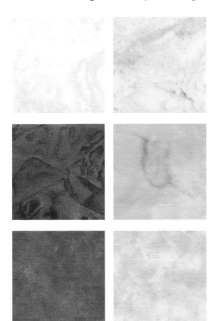

Tone-on-tone fabrics

White-on-Whites

White-on-white fabrics are solids with a printed design that has been applied to the fabric. To me the design often looks like it has been stamped onto the fabric. When I use these fabrics in my quilts, I usually turn them over, wrong side up. All of the pieces must be turned the same direction. Turning them wrong side up creates a background that is very subtle, and the pattern disruption is hard to see.

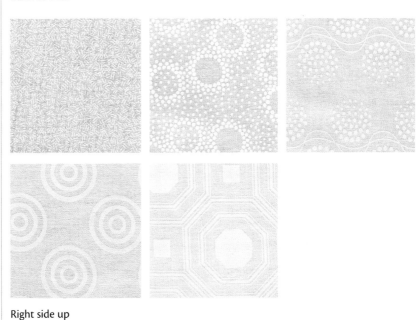

Right side up

Wrong side up

Small Prints

My favorite background fabrics are those that have a small random print. They do in fact have a repeating pattern, but the print is so small and scattered that it is hard to see the repeat. This will allow it to be cut up and pieced back together with no problem in disrupting the pattern of the print.

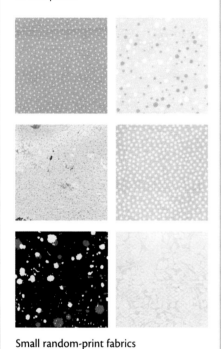

Small random-print fabrics

Main Design Fabrics

When selecting fabrics for your main design, try to keep in mind that many "traditional" art deco designs used very bold, contrasting colors to make a visual statement. It seems as if all the old rules governing the preceding art form, art nouveau, were thrown out the window with a vengeance. Artists of the art nouveau era used muted colors and sinuous, curving designs. This is not to say that your pieces must use bold, contrasting colors, but if you research this art form, I think you will find this is often the case.

I recommend that you keep the number of main design fabrics to between four and eight. My quilt *Deco Cathedral I* has only three colors: black, white, and red. Compare the look with that of *Deco Cathedral II*, which has five colors and looks very different because of the colors and a minor change in the layout of the prints. (Larger photos of these quilts are shown on pages 38 and 42.)

Deco Cathedral I

Deco Cathedral II

If there is going to be a large area such as a symmetrical or an asymmetrical focal point, you might want to select a large floral, abstract, or Asian print for this area. These design elements provide an excellent opportunity to use some of those fabrics that you just can't bring yourself to cut up into small pieces.

Large-print fabrics

Other areas of the quilt lend themselves to more geometric designs, such as squares, triangles, polka dots, and angular patterns. Many art deco designs used these themes in their patterns. These geometric designs will help tie the large aforementioned prints into the whole art deco design of the quilt.

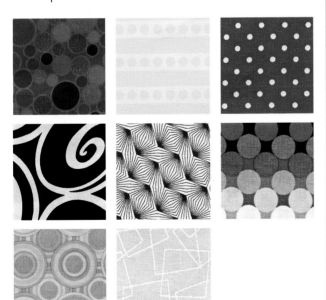

Fabrics with geometric designs

I want to say again that these are my preferences and my preferences alone. If you prefer using other fabrics, then by all means go with what you enjoy.

COLOR SUGGESTIONS

In case you have trouble with the fabric color selection, I would like to make a few suggestions that may help.

First of all, if you are using a large print as a focal point, you can repeat the colors within the print. The people who design these prints are pros when it comes to color. You cannot fail if you do this.

Another possibility is to look on the Internet at art deco items. Clarice Cliff was a famous designer of ceramics in Great Britain, and her pieces are quite reflective of the colors and designs used in this art form.

C&T Publishing has an excellent tool called the 3-in-1 Color Tool, by Joen Wolfrom, which will help you with your color selection process (see page 80). This tool works much better than the standard color wheel that is sold for painting. I highly recommend it.

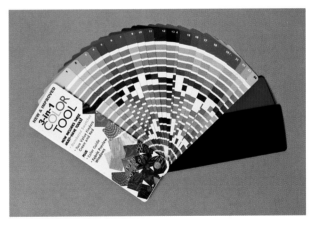

3-in-1 Color Tool

CHAPTER **3**

DESIGN STEPS

ou should always remember: You are the artist. The following guidelines cover some basic design steps to get you on your way to designing your own art quilts.

First of all, I encourage you to make a habit of carrying a pad of paper and pencil, and perhaps even a small digital camera, wherever you go. Second, I encourage you to look closely at everything you come in contact with as you go about your life.

Use the paper, pencil, and camera to record interesting designs and shapes that you see so that they can be used as possible design components for your quilts. Make quick sketches of shapes that interest you. They do not have to be pretty or realistic. These sketches or photos can be used to jog your memory when you start designing. I always think to myself when I see something interesting, "I'll remember that." Guess what—more times than not I would forget.

To get you started on this new creative adventure, I have provided you with some basic and not-so-basic design components in Chapter 7 (pages 70–78). Combine these components or use them on their own to design your first projects. Of course, you could just sit down with some graph paper, a pencil, and an eraser and then sketch your own design. This is the way I usually do it, but most people tend to find this a bit intimidating to begin with.

The following steps are designed to help this process be less intimidating. Don't say, "I can't do this," because it will become a self-fulfilling prophecy.

THE PROCESS: MAKING THE SCALE MOCK-UP

WARNING!

This can become addicting. Proceed at your own risk.

Border Area

First, make a scale mock-up of the quilt you will construct. I say "construct" rather than "piece" because of how these quilts go together.

1. Decide what size you want the quilt top to be. Most quilts I make are wallhanging or lap size. It seems that I'm always planning my next quilt about the time I get halfway through my current project. If I keep my projects in the neighborhood of 60" × 72", I can keep moving on to the next project I have in mind.

For this project let's go with a size of 60" × 76". We have the option of altering the size as we go along, if we so desire.

Use graph paper divided into 8 squares per inch. (Each square is ⅛" × ⅛") For our purposes, ⅛" on the paper mock-up equals 1" on the finished quilt. Thus, one square represents 1"; 3 squares are equal to 3". When I say that something is 2" wide, you will be measuring 2 squares, or ¼".

2. Tape enough sheets of graph paper together to give you at least 60 squares wide by 76 squares high.

I like to allow a few extra squares on each side to give me room for adjustment if necessary as I work on the design.

3. With your ruler, draw a rectangle 60" wide by 76" high in the center of the graph paper.

4. Pin or tape the graph paper to the center of a piece of foamcore board.

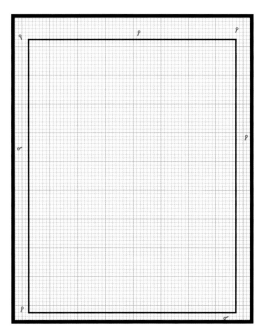

Draw lines, then attach graph paper to foamcore board.

You now have a portable design board similar to a flannel design wall. Pretty cool, huh?

I like to work in whole-inch increments on my designs. To me, this is easier, and easier is good. However, you could work in any increments that look good to you. You would just have to pay more attention to the layout as you progress.

For this exercise I am going to say that the finished fabric strips are 1″, 2″, and 3″ wide (which translates to ⅛″, ¼″, and ⅜″ on the graph paper and ⅛″-, ¼″-, and ⅜″-wide colored construction paper strips). Other widths could be used, depending on your preference. The joy of this technique is the flexibility you have in making changes as your work progresses.

5. If you know what color your background is going to be, you could shade the graph paper lightly with a colored pencil. All we are really trying to do is get a feeling of the layout and color contrast between design elements.

6. Cut some strips of construction paper to the appropriate widths for the border design. The easiest way to do this is with a rotary cutter and a quilt ruler. Remember that I said I was going to work with 1″, 2″, and 3″ fabric strips for the actual quilt, so select a construction paper color or colors and cut 6 paper strips each: ⅛″, ¼″, and ⅜″ wide.

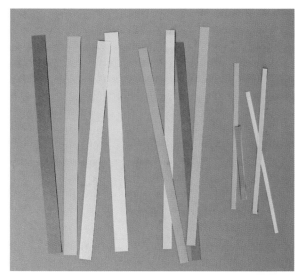

Cut paper strips.

NOTE

For the remainder of this chapter, reference to the widths of the strips represent the cut-paper widths, not the finished fabric widths in the constructed quilt.

For this exercise we'll be using some design components from Chapter 7 (pages 70–78) as a starting point from which to build. I suggest that you photocopy these pages so that you can spread them out in front of you for inspiration. You can also cut them up and lay them together for additional ideas. Note that all of the design components in this quilt are shown on page 71.

7. Start by building the outside border of the quilt. Cut short paper strips and pin them to the graph paper that is pinned to the foamcore board.

I've started my design on the outside edge of the drawn rectangle. You could also come in 1–2 squares if you like the look of that better. Don't be afraid to experiment with the lengths of the strips and the shapes of the ends of the strips. In my example, I've made one side a little different from the other just to give you an idea of how a minor change can make a big difference in the overall look.

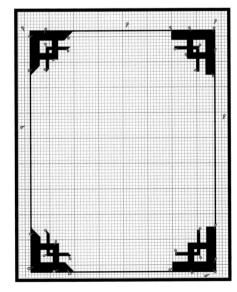

Trim and pin strips to graph paper.

8. I added some ⅛″ strips to the corner elements.

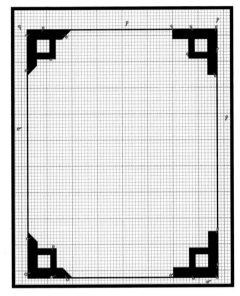

Add more strips.

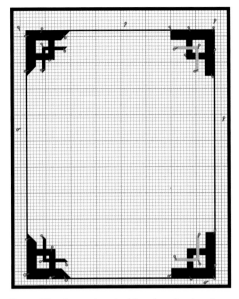

Some ⅛″ strips replaced with colored strips. A small adjustment can make a significant impact.

Once we have the corners in place, we can start thinking about joining the corners with some kind of design along the sides, or maybe we want to let the corners stand on their own. Remember, changes can be made at any time during the evolution of the mock-up on the design board.

9. I connected the corners with some very elemental shapes: straight strips. The ¼″ strips are offset to try to create a feeling of asymmetry in the "border."

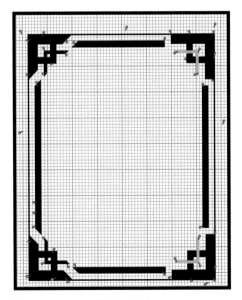

Connect corners with simple shapes.

Our mock-up looks okay so far, but it's a little on the ho-hum side. Let's see if we can dress it up by adding another very simple shape to the mix.

10. I think that by adding some triangles to the ¼" strips along the sides, a whole new level of interest has been achieved. You could change the look of the borders by reversing the placement of the triangles or changing the colors of the strips.

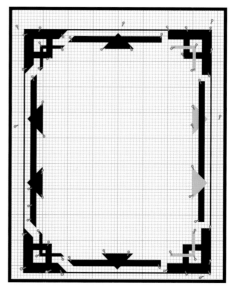

Some triangles replaced with colored triangles to increase the visual interest

For the time being, I'm going to say that I'm satisfied with the layout of the design. I'll decide on the color of the ⅛" strips and the triangles later on when I create a fabric mock-up (page 22). As we add more design elements with paper, I'll refer to them by width and color, just to be clear.

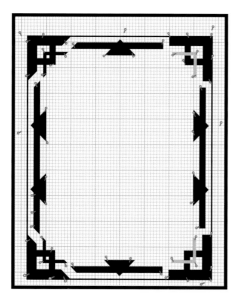

Add some triangles.

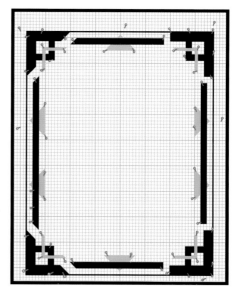

Designed border area

Interior Area

Now it's time to move to the interior of the quilt design.

1. I added a ⅜"-wide yellow rectangular frame inside the outer border.

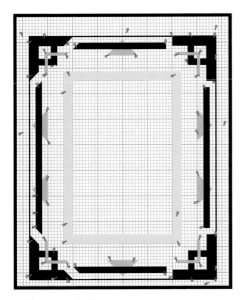

Add rectangular frame.

Unfortunately, it looks like a picture frame to me. We want something different than a run-of-the-mill border! But, let's not totally discard the frame idea. Instead let's dress it up a little.

2. First, temporarily remove the ⅜" yellow frame we just put in place.

From the inside of the lower left corner element, I'm going to count over 1 square and up 1 square of the mock-up; you can put a pin there as a marker pin if you like. On the upper left corner element, I'm going to repeat this process, except this time I will only go down 1 square and not move over. I have pinned a ¼"-wide lavender strip in place both horizontally and vertically, starting where I put my marking pin. The lengths of the horizontal strips are not important at this point. All I'm trying to do is set up an asymmetrical design that will tie in to the border area.

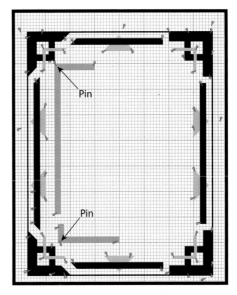

Place pins to position vertical and horizontal strips.

3. I'm now going to move in 3 squares from the side and 2 squares from the ends and put the frame back in place on 3 sides, with the top and bottom strips being too long.

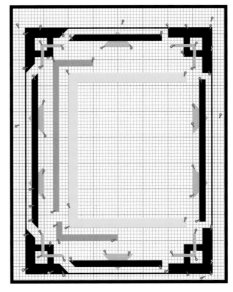

Reposition ⅜" yellow frame.

About now you're saying, "Big deal. He added some ¼" strips and put the same old picture frame back in, only a little smaller." Wait, I'm not done yet!

4. Next I will connect those floating ¼" lavender paper strips to the left side of the ⅜" yellow frame.

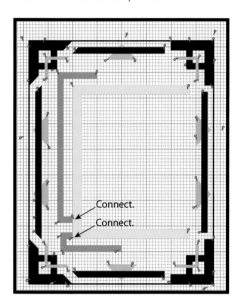

Connect strips.

5. Finish the ⅜" yellow frame so that it is centered on the quilt top.

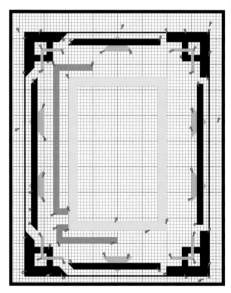

Finish frame.

There's a pretty big open area inside the frame that screams for some asymmetrical design elements to act as a focal point for the whole design. Referring to the design elements (page 71), I'm going to pull a few out and mix it up just a little.

6. In the lower right corner, I'm going to put a large quarter-circle.

I see a large floral print in this area. You know the one I am talking about. It's the piece that you can't bring yourself to cut up because it's so pretty.

7. Next I'll join a couple of half-circles with 2 pink strips, each ⅜" wide.

These curved elements will help soften the bold geometric designs throughout the rest of the mock-up. I offset this design element 2 squares off-center to help balance the design elements within the ⅜" yellow frame. At the same time, I'm going to bring the ¼" lavender strip back into the ⅜" yellow frame, so that it looks like it's going under the large quarter-circle that's inside the frame.

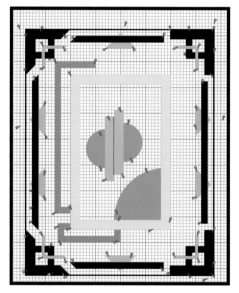

Add design elements.

8. The two ⅜" pink strips that split the half-circles are rather boring to my eye. Let's add a couple diagonal strips to each one to help create a little visual interest.

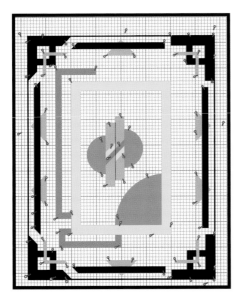

Include diagonal strips.

The design is starting to come together, but the right side is looking a little lonely compared with the left side. We also have some pretty large open areas in the center of the mock-up around the asymmetric design elements.

9. I added some ¼" lavender strips to the right side (and a few to the left side). At the same time, I'm going to make these strips appear as if they run under the ⅜" yellow frame and project into the center of the design.

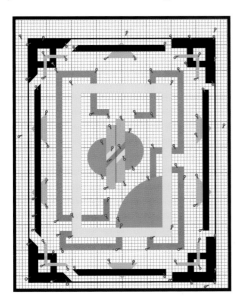

Add ¼" lavender strips for balance.

10. This looks good, but the ¼" lavender strips just kind of dangle there in the center space, so I added some small design elements and called it done.

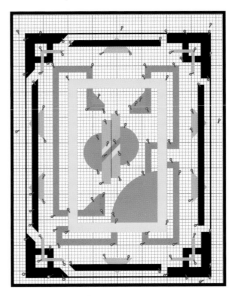

Finish with triangles.

We now have a totally original design that forces the viewer's eyes to move around the whole quilt without resting in any one place too long.

Fabric Mock-up

I did a mock-up of the design using the fabrics that I've chosen for this project. This is easily accomplished by pinning fabric strips to a foamcore board as we did with the paper strips. I also cut all the ends of the black border strips at a 45° angle.

By now, I think you'll see why I warned you about this being addictive. It's like being a kid again, when we played with colored construction paper, cutting out odd shapes and laying them out in different designs. Just one little change—adding or removing a strip or shape—will change the appearance of your design.

I encourage you to get busy and create some designs of your own. Don't be afraid to play around. You'll know when something looks good to you. If you don't like something, just change it.

After you have your design done, put it in another room and don't look at it for at least a couple of hours or more; then go back and appraise it with a fresh set of eyes.

Another good method is to take a digital photo of the mock-up. For some reason looking at a photo is different from looking at the real thing. (If you don't believe me, look at yourself in a mirror and then look at yourself in a photograph.)

If your mock-up looks good, then you can move on to the next phase. If something looks out of place, don't be afraid to change it. When you're finally satisfied with your design, use a glue pen to glue all of the paper pieces to the graph paper. I know that I'm harping on this, but *you are the artist*. Your design should make you feel good. Don't worry about what others may think of it. It'll probably shock some traditional quilters, and that's okay. You're creating, not just following a well-worn path.

In Chapter 4, you'll learn how to piece your original work of art.

Fabric mock-up

PIECING SEQUENCE

Now that the design is complete, it is time to map out how to piece it. Don't be intimidated by this. It's not as hard as it looks at first glance. I'll break the process down into bite-size pieces that are very manageable. Any quilt design can be divided into large "blocks" that can be broken down and pieced.

This process is kind of like taking a picture and turning it into a puzzle that must be put back together. What we need to do is decide on the size and shape of the puzzle pieces. There are many possibilities, but the objective is to find a sequence that is easy and doable.

I will offer some tips and guidelines that seem to work well for me. The guidelines should help with breaking down the whole design into workable chunks.

Tips will cover sewing, yardage estimation, keeping track of fabric pieces, and the dreaded inset or Y-seam (should there be no way around it).

The design developed in the previous chapter will be broken down into large blocks, which will then be divided into smaller blocks. The smaller blocks will be broken down into sets, which will be made by sewing individual pieces together or to previously made sets.

Now let's get started. The following process can be applied to any design you come up with.

When I look at this design, I see a large, center rectangle with a 3" frame (⅜" wide on the graph paper mock-up), surrounded by an outer border.

TIP

For our graph paper drawings, 1 square = 1 inch in the quilt. Each of the pieces on the graph represents finished measurements in the quilt. We'll need to add $1/4$" seam allowances before cutting out the pieces. For example, a finished rectangle measuring 2" × 4" in the quilt would need to be cut out $2^1/_2$" × $4^1/_2$" to allow for a $1/4$" seam allowance on each side.

The borders are pieced first, and then sewn to the center section later, after it is constructed. The outside border is broken into individual elements: top and bottom borders, side borders, and corner blocks.

My initial approach will be to sew the top and bottom borders to the central rectangle. The corner blocks will be sewn to the side borders, which will then be added to complete the quilt top.

If I find myself "boxed in" with my initial approach, I will just come up with a different plan of attack. If you find that your initial approach to adding the border cannot easily be pieced, then you may have to change the way the borders are pieced.

CASCADE by Don Linn, 60″ × 72″

PIECING THE BORDER

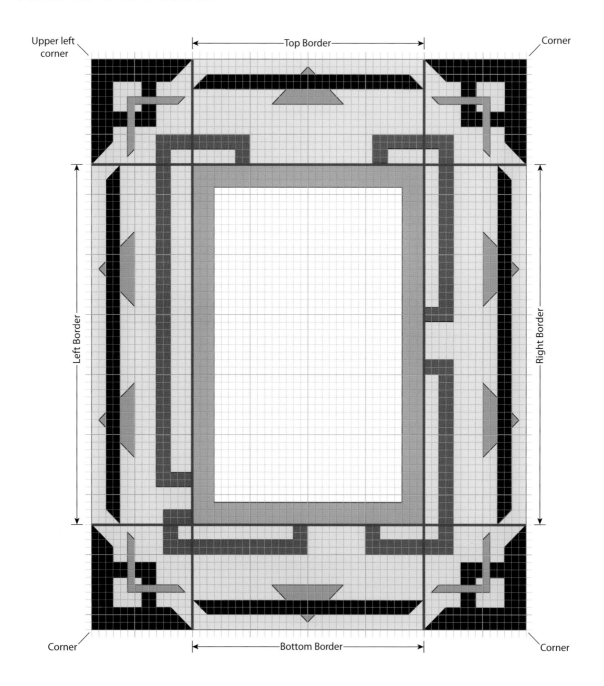

Upper left corner · Top Border · Corner

Left Border · Right Border

Corner · Bottom Border · Corner

NOTE

Upper left corner is slightly different than the remaining corners. The maroon strip extends one square further to the outside. Similarly, the top and bottom borders, as well as the left and right borders, vary in the placement of the maroon strips.

Corner Blocks

There are three corner blocks that are identical and one that is a slight variation.

1. Break down and label the individual pieces. Typically, I use small sticky notes as labels. Identify each piece made from the same fabric with the same letter: A1, A2, A3, and so forth. *This step is very important to the whole process.*

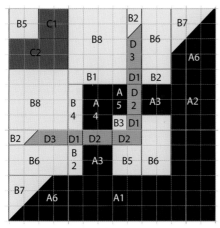

Make 3.

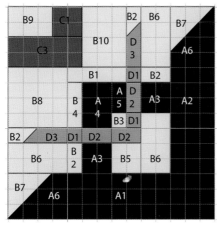

Make 1.

Label individual pieces.

2. Make a list of the cut size of each piece, the ID label, and the quantity required.

CORNER BLOCK COMPONENTS

Piece ID	Number to cut	Size	Total square inches
A1	4	3½″ × 7½″	105
A2	4	3½″ × 10½″	147
A3	8	2½″ × 2½″	50
A4	4	2½″ × 3½″	35
A5	4	1½″ × 2½″	15
A6	8	3½″ × 4½″	126
		TOTAL Fabric A:	478
B1	4	1½″ × 4½″	27
B2	16	1½″ × 2½″	60
B3	4	1½″ × 1½″	9
B4	4	1½″ × 3½″	21
B5	7	2½″ × 2½″	43.75
B6	12	2½″ × 4½″	135
B7	8	3½″ × 3½″	98
B8	7	4½″ × 4½″	141.75
B9	1	2½″ × 3½″	8.75
B10	1	3½″ × 4½″	15.75
		TOTAL Fabric B:	560
C1	4	2½″ × 2½″	25
C2	3	2½″ × 4½″	33.75
C3	1	2½″ × 5½″	13.75
		TOTAL Fabric C:	72.50
D1	12	1½″ × 1½″	27
D2	12	1½″ × 2½″	45
D3	8	1½″ × 3½″	42
		TOTAL Fabric D:	114

Piecing

You will start by building small blocks or strips that can be joined together into larger blocks. Try starting in the center of the block or the end of a strip and build in sections. Determine the piecing sequence you will use.

Make a piecing sequence list to keep track of your progress.

You can follow along if you are making this project, or you can develop your own sequence if you are making your own design. This sequence is just one of many different ways of piecing the corner blocks.

1. Sew together the pieces to make Unit 1. A plus sign (+) indicates that the units are to be sewn together. Unit 1 is identical in all four corners. Make 4.

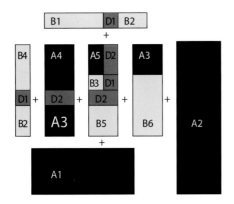

Make 4.

Unit 1 assembly

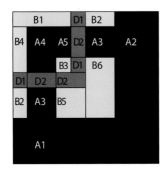

2. Sew together the Step 2 units. Pay close attention to the orientation of the diagonal seam in each unit.

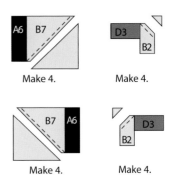

Make 4.   Make 4.

Make 4.   Make 4.

Unit 2 assembly

TIP

To make the breakdown of the piecing sequence easier, cover your mock-up design with a sheet of vinyl (such as Quilter's Vinyl by C&T Publishing, see page 80) and tape it in place. Use a dry-erase pen to draw in the piecing lines. If changes have to be made, the lines can easily be erased and redrawn.

Cover mock-up with Quilter's Vinyl

DIAGONAL PIECING

Use a 45° triangle and pencil to draw a diagonal line on the backside of the square piece of fabric B7, making sure the orientation is correct.

Pin the 2 pieces right sides together along the pencil line. Sew just inside the pencil line on the waste side. Turn and press; trim away the waste.

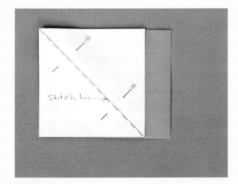

Draw diagonal line.

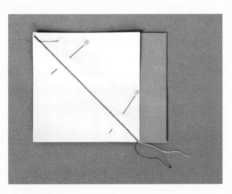

Pin and sew.

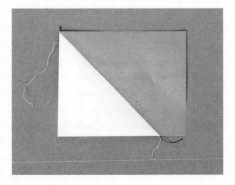

Turn, press, and trim.

3. The assembly process for Unit 3 is the same for each of the corner blocks. However, one Unit 3 in the lower left corner block uses different sized pieces than other Unit 3's. Sew together three Unit 3's and one Unit 3 alternate.

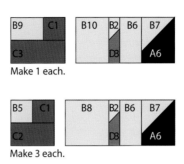

Make 1 each.

Make 3 each.

Make 4.

Unit 3 assembly

4. Sew together Units 1, 2, and 3 to complete the 4 corner blocks.

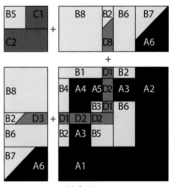

Make 3.

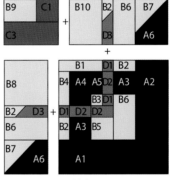

Make 1.

Assemble corner blocks.

Top and Bottom Borders

To piece the top and bottom borders, create manageable units, as we did for the corner block. In this case the units will be sewn together in strip sets. We will start by labeling the individual pieces, as shown below.

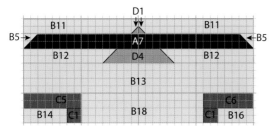

Top border

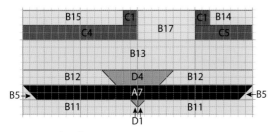

Bottom border
Label individual pieces.

TOP AND BOTTOM BORDER COMPONENTS

Piece ID	Number to cut	Size	Total square inches
A7	2	2½" × 32½"	162.50
		TOTAL Fabric A:	162.50
B5	4	2½" × 2½"	25
B11	4	2½" × 16½"	165
B12	4	2½" × 13½"	135
B13	2	4½" × 32½"	292.50
B14	2	2½" × 6½"	32.50
B15	1	2½" × 14½"	36.25
B16	1	2½" × 5½"	13.75
B17	1	4½" × 8½"	38.25
B18	1	4½" × 17½"	78.75
		TOTAL Fabric B:	817
C1	4	2½" × 2½"	25
C4	1	2½" × 16½"	41.25
C5	2	2½" × 8½"	42.50
C6	1	2½" × 7½"	18.75
		TOTAL Fabric C:	127.50
D1	4	1½" × 1½"	9
D4	2	2½" × 10½"	52.50
		TOTAL Fabric D:	61.50

1. Sew together the strips.

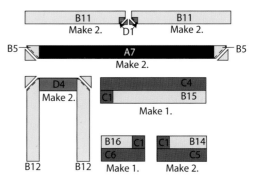

2. Assemble the top and bottom borders.

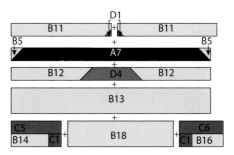

Top border

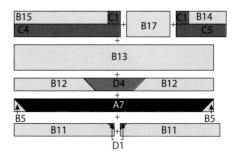

Bottom border

Side Borders

To piece side borders, label each piece and create manageable strip set units, as we did for the top and bottom borders.

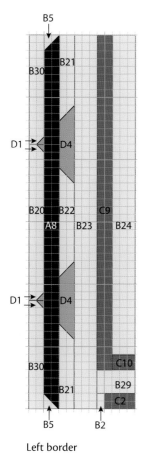

Left border

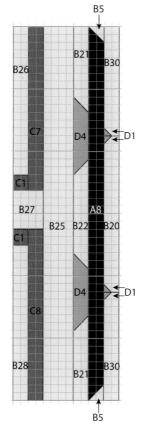

Right border

Label individual pieces.

SIDE BORDER COMPONENTS

Piece ID	Number to cut	Size	Total square inches
A8	2	2½″ × 48½″ *	242.50
TOTAL Fabric A:			**242.50**
B2	1	1½″ × 2½″	3.75
B5	4	2½″ × 2½″	25
B20	2	2½″ × 20½″	102.50
B21	4	2½″ × 11½″	115
B22	2	2½″ × 14½″	72.50
B23	1	3½″ × 48½″ *	169.75
B24	1	3½″ × 41½″ *	145.25
B25	1	4½″ × 48½″ *	218.25
B26	1	2½″ × 19½″	48.75
B27	1	4½″ × 5½″	24.75
B28	1	2½″ × 20½″	51.25
B29	1	3½″ × 5½″	19.25
B30	4	2½″ × 14½″	145
TOTAL Fabric B:			**1,141**
C1	2	2½″ × 2½″	12.50
C2	1	2½″ × 4½″	11.25
C7	1	2½″ × 21½″	53.75
C8	1	2½″ × 22½″	56.25
C9	1	2½″ × 43½″ *	108.75
C10	1	2½″ × 3½″	8.75
TOTAL Fabric C:			**251.25**
D1	8	1½″ × 1½″	18
D4	4	2½″ × 10½″	105
TOTAL Fabric D:			**123**

You may need to piece together two shorter strips to create the longer strips.

1. Sew together the strip set units.

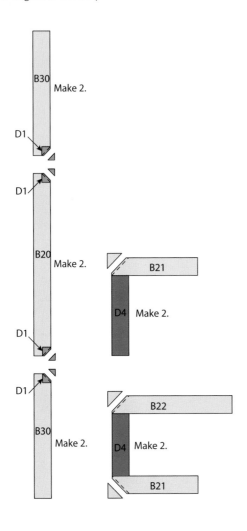

B30 Make 2.

D1

D1

B20 Make 2.

D1

D1

B30 Make 2.

B21

D4 Make 2.

B22

D4 Make 2.

B21

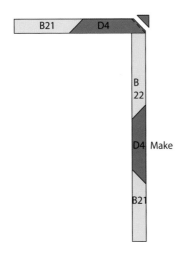

B21   D4

B
22

D4 Make

B21

2. Sew the strip set units together to create the side borders.

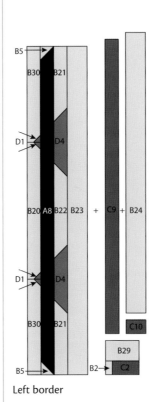

B5

B30 B21

D1   D4

B20 A8 B22 B23   +   C9   +   B24

D1   D4

B30 B21

C10

B5   B2→   B29 / C2

Left border

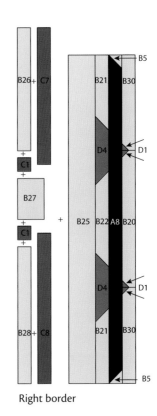

B26 + C7

B21 B30   B5

D4   D1

+
C1
+

B27

+
C1
+

B25 B22 A8 B20

D4   D1

B28 + C8

B21 B30

B5

Right border

PIECING THE CENTER SECTION AND ADDING THE BORDER

The center section is no different from what we have already done with the border and corner blocks, except for insetting the quarter- and half-circles. These are really quite easy to do, and detailed instructions are on pages 55–58.

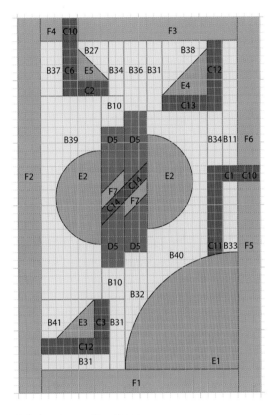

Label center section pieces.

CENTER SECTION COMPONENTS

Piece ID	Number to cut	Size	Total square inches
B10	2	3½″ × 4½″	31.50
B11	1	2½″ × 16½″	41.25
B27	1	4½″ × 5½″	24.75
B31	3	2½″ × 9½″	71.25
B32	1	3½″ × 15½″	54.25
B33	1	2½″ × 24½″	61.25
B34	2	2½″ × 7½″	37.50
B36	1	3½″ × 9½″	33.25
B37	1	3½″ × 7½″	26.25
B38	1	6½″ × 7½″	48.75
B39	1	8½″ × 26½″	225.25
B40	1	8½″ × 33½″	284.75
B41	1	5½″ × 7½″	41.25
		TOTAL Fabric B:	**981.25**
C1	1	2½″ × 2½″	6.25
C2	1	2½″ × 4½″	11.25
C3	1	2½″ × 5½″	13.75
C6	1	2½″ × 7½″	18.75
C10	2	2½″ × 3½″	17.50
C11	1	2½″ × 26½″	66.25
C12	2	2½″ × 9½″	47.50
C13	1	2½″ × 6½″	16.25
C14	2	1½″ × 8″	24
		TOTAL Fabric C:	**221.50**
D5	4	3½″ × 14½″	203
		TOTAL Fabric D:	**203**
E1	1	19″ × 19″	361
E2	2	8″ × 16″	256
E3	1	5½″ × 5½″	30.25
E4	1	6½″ × 6½″	42.25
E5	1	4½″ × 4½″	20.25
		TOTAL Fabric E:	**709.75**
F1	1	3½″ × 26½″	92.75
F2	1	3½″ × 48½″	169.75
F3	1	3½″ × 21½″	75.25
F4	1	3½″ × 3½″	12.25
F5	1	3½″ × 27½″	96.25
F6	1	3½″ × 19½″	68.25
F7	2	1½″ × 8″	24
		TOTAL Fabric F:	**538.50**

Center Section Construction

1. Inset the half-circles in pieces B39 and B40. The half-circles will have a finished radius of 6". Refer to pages 55–58 for complete instructions.

2. Cut off 1 end of each D5 strip at a 45° angle.

3. Sew F7 to C14 along the long sides.

4. Center F7/C14 on the 45° edge of D5. Make sure they are properly oriented in relation to your mock-up.

5. Sew F7/C14 to D5. Press and trim excess F7/C14 from each side.

6. Pin and sew the remaining D5 piece to the end of the F7/C14/D5 assembly.

7. Repeat Steps 3–6 to make the other F7/C14/D5 assembly, noting the reversed position of F7 and C14.

TIP

When the two pieces are pinned together, you should have a "V" on each side where the pieces overlap. There will also be a small "dog ear" sticking up. The distance from the edge of the dog-eared fabric to the bottom of the V should be equal to your seam allowance. Your seamline should begin and end in the bottom of the V.

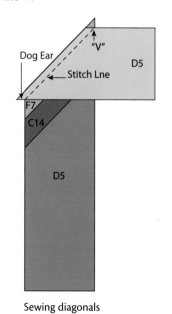

Sewing diagonals

---

8. Press, making sure everything aligns properly.

9. Locate the center of these assemblies, measure 9¼" to each end, and trim.

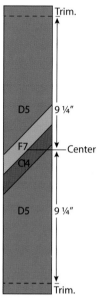

Trim to length.

10. Assemble the triangle units as shown below.

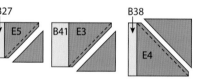

11. Assemble the parts of the center section.

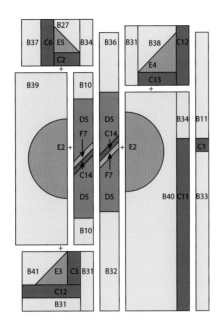

12. Refer to pages 55–58 for how to insert the quarter-circle. The quarter-circle will have a finished radius of 16". It must be inserted before the borders (F1, F2, and so forth) are attached.

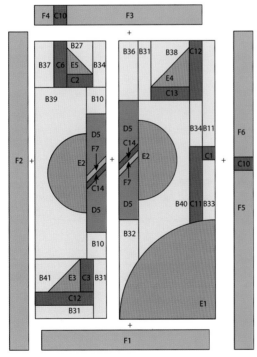

Add quarter-circle and inner borders to center section.

Add the Borders

1. Sew the top and bottom borders to the center section.

2. Sew the corner blocks to the side borders and add to complete the quilt top.

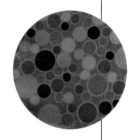

ESTIMATING YARDAGE

There are a couple ways of estimating the yardage required for these unique quilts. Since there are no common blocks to the whole quilt, it is not possible to calculate the yardage of a block and then multiply it times the number of blocks in the quilt.

Method 1

1. Draw a cutting diagram of all the pieces of each type of fabric.

2. Referring to the illustration below, add up the total length of fabric needed, in inches (25½″ is required for the A fabrics in the corner blocks, top, bottom, and side borders). Divide this number by 36″ to get the yardage needed: 0.71 yard (¾ yard). This is not very difficult for fabrics with a limited number of pieces.

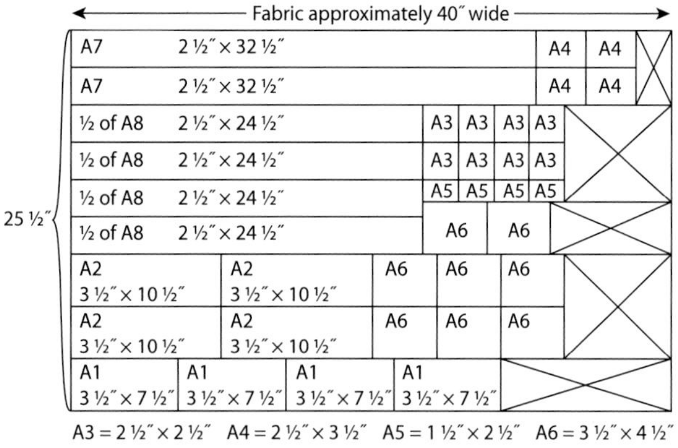

Fabric approximately 40″ wide
25 ½″
A7 2 ½″ × 32 ½″ A4 A4
A7 2 ½″ × 32 ½″ A4 A4
½ of A8 2 ½″ × 24 ½″ A3 A3 A3 A3
½ of A8 2 ½″ × 24 ½″ A3 A3 A3 A3
½ of A8 2 ½″ × 24 ½″ A5 A5 A5 A5
½ of A8 2 ½″ × 24 ½″ A6 A6
A2 3 ½″ × 10 ½″ A2 3 ½″ × 10 ½″ A6 A6 A6
A2 3 ½″ × 10 ½″ A2 3 ½″ × 10 ½″ A6 A6 A6
A1 3 ½″ × 7 ½″ A1 3 ½″ × 7 ½″ A1 3 ½″ × 7 ½″ A1 3 ½″ × 7 ½″
A3 = 2 ½″ × 2 ½″ A4 = 2 ½″ × 3 ½″ A5 = 1 ½″ × 2 ½″ A6 = 3 ½″ × 4 ½″

Cutting diagram

Method 2

The second method involves a little guesstimation. Multiply the length times the width of each piece to give you the square inches per piece. Multiply the result times the number of pieces for each size; add all results together and divide by 1,440. This result will give you the yardage needed. I usually figure my waste to be 30%. To add in the waste, multiply the result of the calculation by 1.30. This will give you a good approximation of the yardage needed.

NOTE

1 yard of fabric based on a 40″ bolt width has 1,440 square inches (36″ × 40″ = 1,440 sq. inches/yard)

Fabric (A)

A1: 3½″ × 7½″ × 4 pieces = 105 square inches

A2: 3½″ × 10½″ × 4 pieces = 147 square inches

A3: 2½″ × 2½″ × 8 pieces = 50 square inches

A4: 2½″ × 3½″ × 4 pieces = 35 square inches

A5: 1½″ × 2½″ × 4 pieces = 15 square inches

A6: 3½″ × 4½″ × 8 pieces = 126 square inches

A7: 2½″ × 32½″ × 2 pieces = 162.5 square inches

A8: 2½″ × 48½″ × 2 pieces = 242.5 square inches

Total: 883 square inches

883 square inches divided by 1,440 square inches/square yard of fabric = 0.61 yards

0.61 yards × 1.3 (waste factor) = 0.79 yards

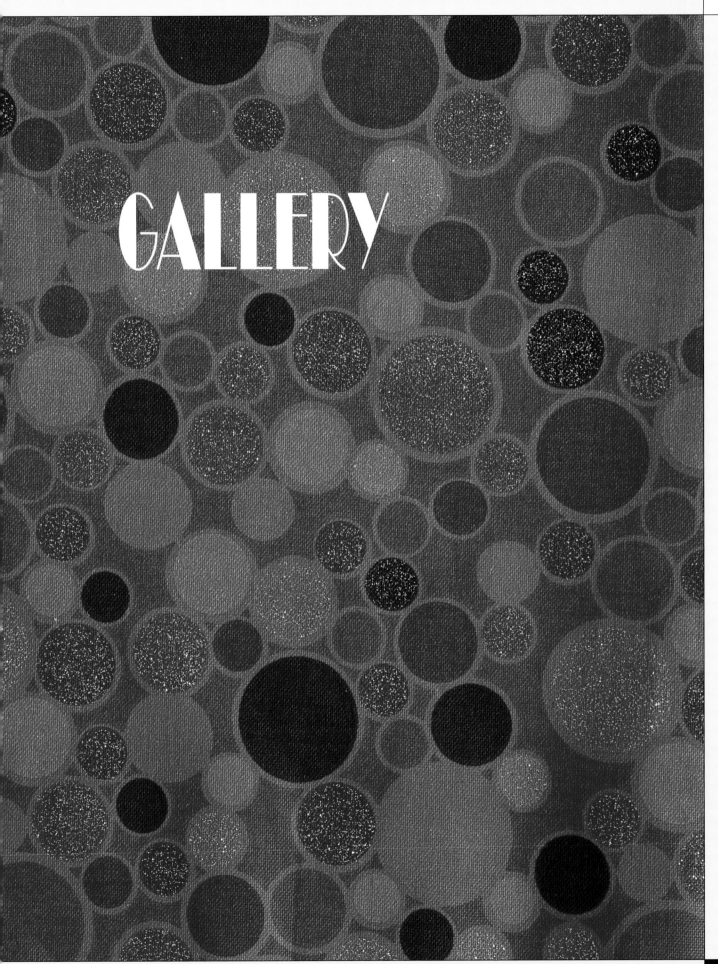

GALLERY

DECO CATHEDRAL II by Don Linn, 46″ × 62½″

SPLIT DECISION by Don Linn, 41″ × 54¹/₂″

XUBERANCE by Don Linn, 48½″ × 62″

DECODANCE by Don Linn, 46″ × 59¹/₂″

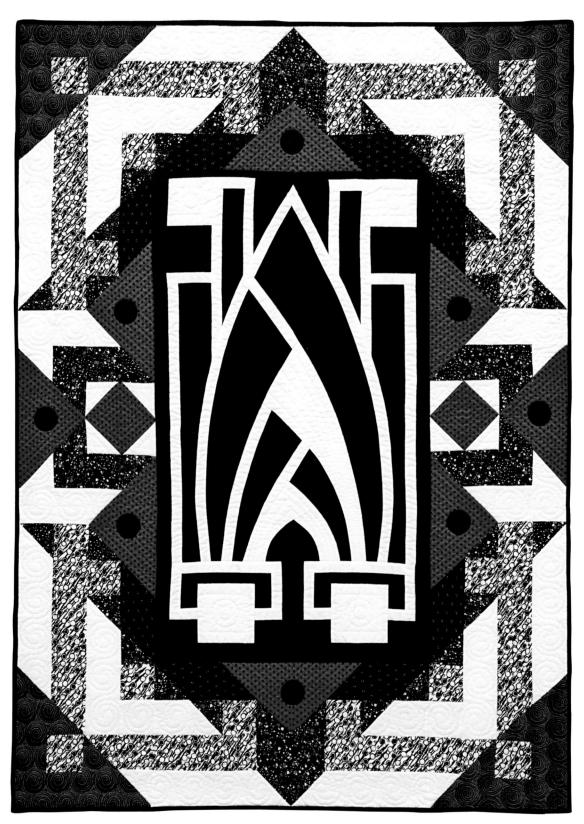

DECO CATHEDRAL I by Don Linn, 45″ × 62″

CALIFORNIA SUNSHINE by Tenna Olsen, 47″ × 64″

ARIZONA SUMMER by Tenna Olsen, 54½″ × 56″

ANYTHING GOES by Fran Brooks, 56" × 72"

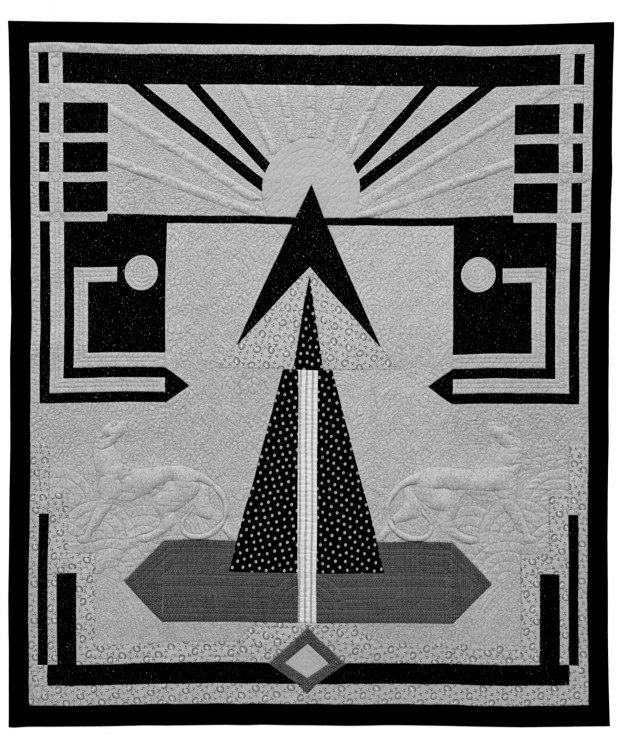

DECO DELIMA by Katherine Fletcher, 47″ × 64″

ART DECO WOW by Merri Caywood, 55½″ × 76″

WALL STREET OCTOBER by Connie Livingston, 38″ × 52″

SUNRISE by Charlotte Uchimura, 48″ × 66″

PHARAOH'S FUN by Sharon McDaniel, 36" × 45"

SERENDIPITY QUILT by Deborah Storz, 48″ × 63″

NO WORRIES ISLAND by Teresa Abbott, 46″ × 61″

DECO CELEBRATION by Louise Harlan Wilson, 48″ × 60″

CHAPTER **5**

CURVED AND INSET SEAM PIECING

CURVED PIECING

Curved piecing can be intimidating to many quilters. I find it to be the most enjoyable form of piecing. It is very rewarding to get those seemingly difficult curves to come together and lie flat.

I am going to give you some tips that will make curved piecing a real pleasure to do.

The first type of curved piecing we will cover will be applicable to the project quilt that we have been working our way through in this book. In the project quilt, quarter- and half-circles are pieced into sections of the quilt top.

Full Circles

To accomplish this type of piecing, you will need poster board, scissors, and a compass. A yardstick compass attachment works great for large circles.

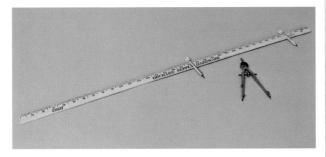

Yardstick compass and small compass

In this example I want to inset an 8"-diameter circle.

NOTE

The diameter of a circle is the measurement across the center of the circle, and the radius is the measurement from the center of the circle to the outside. The radius is half as long as the diameter.

We'll cut a hole in our quilt top (the scary step), and then we'll cut a circle from the fabric that is to be inset. The inset circle has to be bigger than the hole in the quilt; otherwise the circle won't cover the hole. In all cases, the radius of the circle must be ½" larger than the radius of the hole in the quilt top.

1. A finished 8" circle will have a radius of 4", so set your compass at 4¼" (¼" bigger than the finished radius). Place the compass point on one 90° corner of the poster board and draw a quarter-circle.

Draw quarter-circle.

2. Cut out the quarter-circle and label it "Circle."

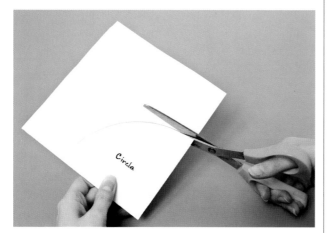

Cut out circle template.

3. Set your compass to 3¾" (¼" smaller than the finished radius), and repeat the above process, but this time, label the quarter-circle "Hole," and set it aside for a moment.

4. Fold your circle fabric in half and press the fold, then in half again and press. You'll have 4 layers of fabric.

Fold and press fabric.

5. Place the template labeled "Circle" on the folded fabric (not the quilt top!), making sure to line up the 90° edges as closely as possible.

Place template on folded fabric.

6. Use a rotary cutter to cut along the curved edge of the template.

7. Repeat the previous process to cut the hole in the quilt top fabric: Fold the quilt top fabric area for the circle to be inset in half and press, then fold in half again and press. Place the template labeled "Hole" on the folded quilt top fabric, making sure to line up the 90° edges as closely as possible. Cut along the curved edge of the template.

8. Lay out the quilt top, right side up, and place the circle on top, right side down, lining up one of the creases in the circle with one of the creases on the hole. Pin together at the crease.

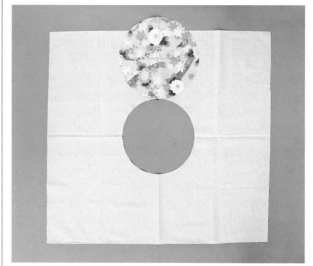

Pin circle to quilt top.

9. Flip the circle through the hole, turn the quilt top over, and hold both pieces so that the circle is closest to your chest and the quilt top is away from you.

Have circle closest to your chest.

10. Line up the remaining creases around the circle and pin at the creases. Use additional pins to ease in the fullness around the circle.

11. Turn the unit over so that the circle is against the sewing machine table; sew the circle to the quilt top. C&T Publishing makes a dandy tool that will really help in easing in any fullness that you may encounter. It is called the Alex Anderson's 4-in-1 Essential Sewing Tool, and it is an invaluable little tool that you will want to keep next to your sewing machine at all times.

Sew circle and quilt top together, using 4-in-1 Essential Sewing Tool to ease in fullness.

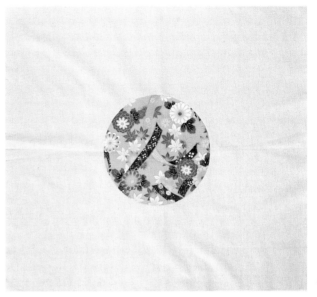

Completed inset circle.

Quarter- and Half-Circles

Quarter-Circles

The quarter-circle in this example will have a finished radius of 6".

These circle sections will be created in much the same way as the full circle, with one minor change when we make our templates. The ¼" seam allowance must be added on the straight edges of the templates.

1. Draw a line ¼" in from both straight sides of the poster board. The lines will intersect at the corner.

Draw ¼" lines.

2. Set the compass to 6¼" (¼" larger than the radius), place the point of the compass on the intersection of the 2 lines, and draw a quarter-circle.

Draw quarter-circle.

3. Cut out this template, and label it "Circle."

4. Place the quarter-circle template on a corner of the quarter-circle fabric (not the quilt top), making sure to line up the 90° edges as closely as possible.

5. Use a rotary cutter to cut along the curved edge of the template.

6. Set the compass to 5¾" (¼" smaller than the radius), and repeat this process. Label this template "Hole."

7. Lay the template labeled "Hole" on the corner of the quilt top where the quarter-circle is to be inserted, and line up the straight edges.

8. Use a rotary cutter to carefully cut around the arc.

9. Pin the quarter-circle in place and sew together.

Half-Circles

A half-circle with a finished radius of 6" is constructed the same way as the quarter-circle; you just have to fold the fabric in half when you cut out the circle part, and then fold the quilt top in half when you cut the hole. Make sure you eliminate the ¼" seam allowance on the side of the template that is on the side of the fold.

Free-form Curves

I call any curve that cannot be drawn with a compass a free-form curve. My quilt *Split Decision* (page 39) utilizes free-form curves. This type of curved piecing is quite easy to do if you follow these steps.

You will need the following tools and supplies; some you will make, and some you can purchase.

- Poster board (enough to draft your full-size pattern twice plus waste)

- Pencils and eraser

- Straight pins (strong ones)

- Quilter's Wonder Wheel (by Collins) or 2 pencils and 3 rubber bands

- Foam craft sheets

- Steel strapping, ½" or ⅝" wide

- Contact cement or another flexible cement that will stick to metal

- Disposable paintbrush, if the cement does not have a brush in container

- Single-edge razor blades or X-acto knife

- Clear adhesive tape

- Double-sided tape

- Disposable rubber gloves

- Handheld calculator

- Carpeted surface or foamcore board for pinning

Free-form curve template supplies

I like to do free-form curved piecing much better than straight piecing—I am only limited by my imagination.

I have drawn an example of a design that I want to turn into a one-of-a-kind quilt.

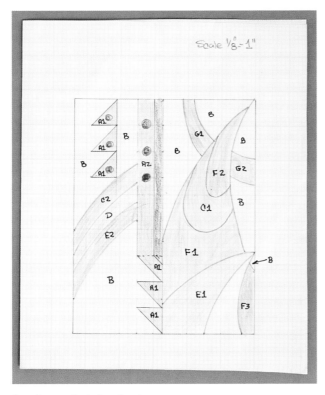

Free-form quilt design sketch

You will need to develop a full-sized pattern to piece the free-form design. Many of the piecing sequence steps are covered in Chapter 4 (pages 24–36). In this chapter, we will only concentrate on curved piecing.

Adjustable-Curve Construction

An adjustable curve must be made before the full-size pattern can be drafted. You can purchase one or use the directions here to make your own.

Adjustable Curve

1. Cut the foam sheets into strips a little wider than the steel strapping. Cut enough strips to equal 3 to 4 times the length of the piece of strapping. A little too much is better than too little.

Cut foam strips.

2. Set up a work area for gluing. Gluing can be somewhat messy, so put down some newspaper or a sheet of plastic to contain the mess.

3. Carefully read the instructions on the glue container and follow all safety precautions listed.

4. Put on your gloves and then glue 3 to 4 layers of the foam strips to one side of the strapping material. Stagger the seams of the foam strips between layers.

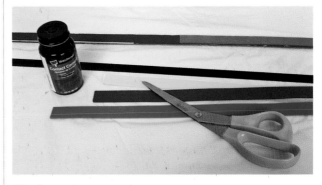

Glue foam strips to strapping.

5. When the glue has cured, trim away any excess foam with a single-edge razor blade or an X-acto knife so that the edges are as smooth and even with the edge of the strapping as possible. Your adjustable curve is now finished.

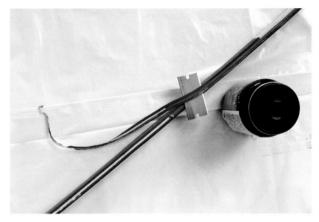

Trim adjustable curve.

Pattern Construction

1. Tape together enough sheets of the poster board to make one sheet large enough to draw your design full size.

2. Calculate the scale relationship between your sketch and the finished size of your quilt top. This is really quite simple. Measure the width of your sketch and the width of the full-size design that you want. In this case, I want my full-size design to be 42″ wide. With a ruler I determine that my sketch is 5¼″ wide.

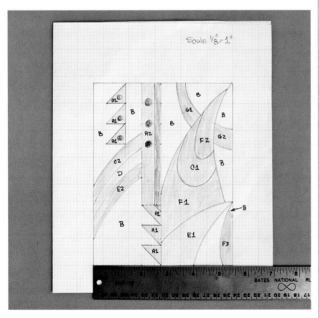

Measure sketch width.

Divide the full-size dimensions by the sketched dimensions to determine the enlargement ratio. In this case, I'm dividing 42 by 5.25. The result of this calculation is 8. This means that the finished design is 8 times bigger than the sketch.

3. Lay the poster board on a carpeted surface. If a carpeted surface is not available, a piece of foamcore board can be placed under the immediate area that will be worked on. This board can be repositioned as needed to work in different areas.

4. Start working on the lower right corner of the full-size pattern. Measure up from the lower right corner of the sketch to where the curve intersects the right side. On the sketch, this measures about 2⅝″.

Keeping in mind that the full-size quilt top will be 8 times as big as the sketch, multiply 8 times 2⅝″, or 2.625″, to get a result of 21″. Do the same calculation across the bottom to get a result of 3″. Place a mark at 3″ and 21″ on the poster board sheet in the appropriate places.

Calculate and transfer measurements from sketch to poster board.

5. Stand the adjustable curve on edge and place a straight pin through the foam and through the 21″ mark on the poster board. Push the pin completely through the carpet or foamcore board. Be sure to leave about 6″ of the adjustable curve sticking out beyond the edge of the poster board.

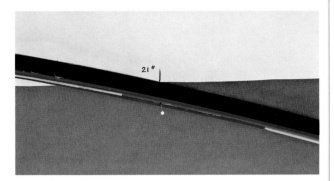

Place pin through all layers.

6. If an exact match of the curve on the sketch is desired, additional measurements up and across the curve on the sketch will have to be taken and transferred to the poster board. (I am usually not that picky on designs such as this project.) Gently bend the adjustable curve until a curve that is pleasing to the eye is generated.

7. Make sure that the adjustable curve crosses the 3″ mark on the edge of the poster board, and then put in a straight pin as before. Put additional pins through the foam all along the curve to securely anchor the adjustable curve. Once the curve is anchored, use a pencil to draw a line on the poster board along the metal edge of the adjustable curve. Continue this process until the whole design is completed.

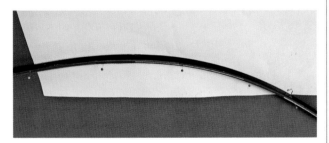

Pin curve to poster board.

8. At roughly 4″ intervals all along each curve, draw a perpendicular line through the curve.

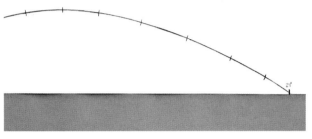

Draw perpendicular lines.

9. Label each piece of the full-size design with an alphanumeric code. The same color fabric will have the same letter identification. For example, the background pieces would be labeled as B1, B2, B3, and so forth.

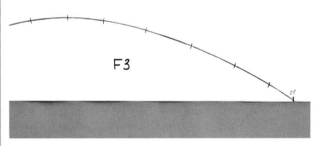

Label pattern pieces.

10. Cut the pieces apart along the pencil lines. Use double-sided tape or a stapler to attach these pieces to another piece of poster board. Be sure to leave at least ¼″ all the way around the cutout template.

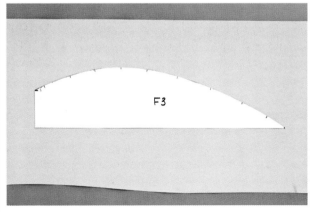

Attach template to poster board.

Template Construction

The next step is to make cut-to-size templates with the seam allowance added to each piece.

There are a couple of tools that can be used to add seam allowances to our templates.

Collins sells a tool called the Quilter's Wonder Wheel. It is a small brass disk with a hole in its center. A sharp pencil is placed in the hole, and it is rolled around the edge of the finished-size templates, which have been attached to another piece of poster board as described in Step 10 on page 61. The small hole in the center is ¼" in from the outside edge of the wheel. This adds the ¼" seam allowance.

The other way of adding a ¼" seam allowance is to use two pencils that are held together with rubber bands. The only problem with this method is that it gives you a slightly wider seam allowance than the wheel does. This can be compensated for by wrapping a rubber band around one pencil before the two pencils are joined together by a second and third rubber band. This places the tips of the pencils just slightly closer together. Roll the rubber band down the pencil to adjust the distance between the pencil points.

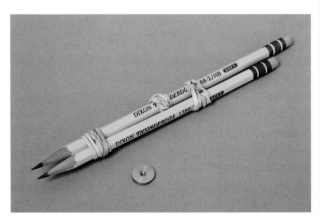

Quilter's Wonder Wheel and the pencil set-up

1. Trace around the finished-size templates, and then project the perpendicular lines across the lines that you just drew.

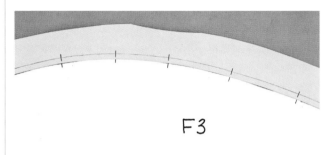

F3

Trace around templates and extend lines.

2. Use paper-cutting scissors to cut along the drawn line, which represents the outside of the seam allowance. The templates are now ready to use.

Fabric Cutting and Sewing

1. Lay the template on a piece of fabric and carefully cut around the template with a rotary cutter. (I like using the small, 28mm cutter for this cutting process. I can see what I am doing better than with the larger sizes, and I feel like I also have more control.) Don't worry too much about the straight of the grain, since everything is on the bias to some extent.

Cut fabric.

2. Before the template is moved, take a small pair of sharp scissors and snip through the template and fabric on the perpendicular lines. When making the snips, be very careful not to snip too deep. Try to go no deeper than ⅛" to avoid potential holes in the quilt top. I like to refer to this as my GPS System (Good Piecing Snip System). These snips are going to make piecing curved seams very easy.

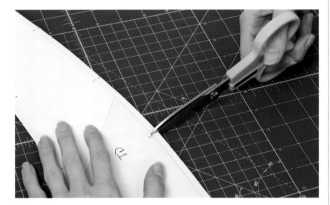

Make snips on perpendicular lines.

Once the pieces are cut out, it's time to pin the pieces together and sew them. I'm going to go over a couple of things that will make the piecing process quite easy to do.

3. Hold a template up in front of you. The edge that is pointing up will look like a hill or a valley. If you rotate the template 180°, you will see just the opposite—a valley or a hill.

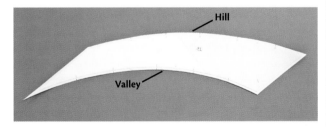

Identify hill or valley side of template.

> ### TIP
>
> To make the piecing easier, hold the piece closest to your chest with the "hill" pointing up. You will be pinning along this hill edge. The piece on the opposite side will have the valley edge pointing up.

Hill edge on top

4. The ends of the pieces will have a dog ear and a V at each end where they overlap. The alignment and pinning of the ends were covered in Chapter 4 (page 34).

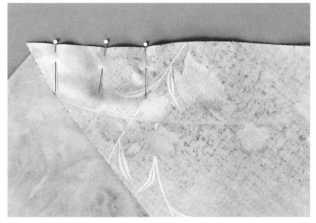

Overlap ends of curved fabric pieces, and pin.

5. After pinning the ends, pin the middle, matching the perpendicular snips you made in each piece.

6. After the pinning is done, sew the pieces together. To make the sewing easier, place the hill side of the pinned assembly against the machine table and the valley side facing up. Sew end to end. Press the seam the way it wants to go, to reduce bulk.

7. Continue sewing the pieces together, following the piecing sequence we developed earlier.

INSET SEAMS

Most of my art deco quilts would require me to do many inset seams if I didn't cheat. By cheating, I mean that I plan my cutting and piecing sequence, so I'm usually able to avoid this type of seam.

Try to make fabric selections so that seamlines within fabric sections are less noticeable. To my eye, small, random prints work the best for backgrounds.

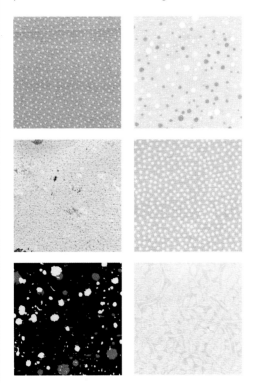

Best background fabric choices

An inset block requires you to change the direction you are sewing within the block.

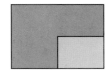

Block with inset seam

The simplest way around this is to add a seam to the block.

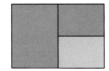

Seam added to block to prevent sewing inset seam

To create a true inset seam, you will only need two pieces of fabric.

1. Cut the large, odd-shaped piece of fabric to the shape and size determined by your graph paper design, adding seam allowances. Then, cut the piece to be inset oversize. Lay out the pieces.

Cut fabric pieces.

2. Locate the inside corner of the piece to be inset. Turn this piece over and draw a 45° line from this corner toward the inside of the piece. Make the line about ½" long and just dark enough so that you can see it.

Draw 45° line.

3. Place the piece to be inset on top of the large piece with the cutout. Line up 1 edge of each piece. Position the piece being inset so that the other edge overlaps ¼" plus your seam allowance. This should add up to a scant ½". Pin the aligned edges together and sew. Stop your seamline when you reach the 45° line, making sure your needle is in the down position.

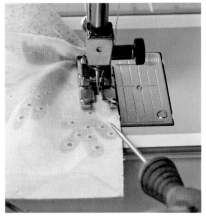

Pin and sew first leg of seam.

4. Raise the presser foot and turn the bottom piece 90° so that the unsewn side is in the position to be sewn. Use your 4-in-1 Essential Sewing Tool to poke the bunched-up fabric behind the needle out of the way; then line up the edge of the top piece of fabric right in the area of the needle. There will be a hump of fabric just to the left of the needle. Use your sewing tool to push this out of the way.

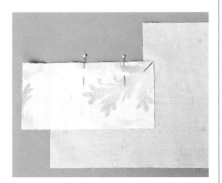

Turn and align pieces with 4-in-1 Essential Sewing Tool.

5. Use your free hand and the 4-in-1 Essential Sewing Tool to keep the 2 pieces of fabric aligned as you sew. Do not pin these edges together.

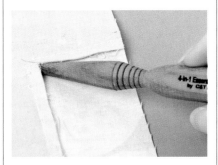

Sewing second leg of seam.

6. Turn the piece over and use the 4-in-1 Essential Sewing Tool to poke out the corner to make it as sharp as possible.

Sharpen corner with 4-in-1 Essential Sewing Tool.

7. Press the seams toward the inset piece.

Press seams.

8. Trim the edges of the inset piece to finish your block.

Trim edges square.

CHAPTER 6

QUILTING IDEAS AND TIPS

I began my adventure in quilting as a machine quilter about fourteen years ago. At the time I couldn't tell a quilt from a turnip. I just jumped in and taught myself how to do what I do.

What I want to do here is to give you a few of my thoughts on how I go about choosing designs with the goal of accentuating my pieced design. Please don't feel that you must do the same thing on your quilts as I do on mine. We all have our own thoughts and opinions about what we do on our quilts. The end use of our quilts is just as different for each of us. I keep almost all of my quilts, and they are never used except to be shown at trunk shows. I'm not saying that what I do is right or wrong, only that it works for me and makes me happy.

The best way I know to accentuate my piecing is to stitch in the ditch and outline stitch around all of the design components.

Stitching in the ditch

I usually do the entire ditch quilting and outlining with clear monofilament thread. I can work faster and with more confidence than when working with colored thread. All this work is done free-motion with the feed dogs lowered. With the feed dogs down, I have the luxury of going in any direction when I come to an intersection of different components.

After I get all of the ditch work done and everything is pretty well locked down, I can then turn my attention to the actual quilting designs that I will do within the design components.

The designs I used on the quilts in this book are not overly ornate or flowery like they are on many of my traditional quilts. Most of the pieced designs are very geometric in nature and that's what I let guide me in choosing my quilting designs. I may decide that my pieced design needs to be softened somewhat. In that case, I might choose some simple, curved quilting designs.

One of my best friends for these geometric designs is a roll of ½-inch masking tape. You can purchase masking tape in narrow widths at paint stores that sell automotive paint. I also usually always keep on hand rolls of ¼-inch and ¾-inch tape. This tape works really well as a guide if you want to quilt a line within a design element, like a triangle or a square.

Quilting line within a triangle

Narrower widths of masking tape also work well as a guide when you are quilting long, gently curved lines.

Use tape as guide for curved lines.

CIRCLES

A drafting template for circles (available from most large office supply stores) is an excellent tool for drawing circles of different diameters. A compass can also be used to draw circles on poster board. The circles can then be cut out and used as templates.

To quilt overlapping circles, you should map out a quilting route so that you don't have to quilt individual circles one at a time.

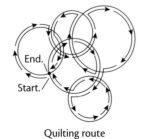

Quilting route

SQUARES, RECTANGLES, AND TRIANGLES

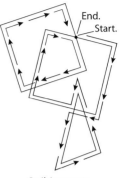

Quilting route

Any shape template can be made from poster board. Squares, rectangles, and triangles can be sewn individually or in combinations. Map out a quilting route so that you don't have to quilt individual shapes one at a time.

TRANSFER DESIGNS

Another thing that I like to do is pull designs from other sources such as fabric prints, copyright-free books, and sketches that I create myself. To do this I use an easy-to-make transfer tool.

Transfer-Tool Supplies

- Embroidery hoop
- Fine mesh tulle fabric (what wedding veils are made from)
- Permanent marking pen
- Scissors
- Design of your choice
- Suitable quilt marking tool *

* The proper marking tool is one that will make a visible mark on the quilt and then be removed with relative ease. The most suitable tool will depend on the color of the fabric and whether or not you are willing to wash your quilt after the quilting is complete.

Transfer-tool supplies

Transfer-Tool Construction

1. Photocopy or draw your design on paper to the size that you want to transfer to your quilt.

Quilting design

2. Put a piece of tulle in the hoop and stretch it as tightly as possible.

3. Lay the hoop on the design, with the tulle resting on the design.

Tulle on design

4. Trace over the design with the permanent marking pen. (Now put this pen out of reach so that you don't take the chance of marking on your quilt with it.)

Trace over design.

5. Position the hoop on the quilt where you want the design to be and trace over the design with the marking device of your choice (*not* the permanent marking pen).

Place hoop on quilt top and trace design with removable marking tool.

6. Remove the hoop. The finished quilt design is ready to be layered and quilted.

Marked quilt top

CHAPTER **7**

DESIGN COMPONENTS

he intent of this chapter is to provide you with some tools that will help spark your imagination when designing your quilts.

On the following pages you will find a series of geometric shapes. Use some of these shapes to help you design your own art deco quilt. The project quilt covered in Chapters 3 and 4 (pages 15–36) was designed by combining the shapes shown on page 72.

There are many other different and distinct designs you could make from these basic shapes. My design, although quite simple, is still very striking to the viewer.

1. I recommend that you study these pages of the design components before starting your design process.

2. When you find designs or design components you want to use, use scissors or a rotary cutter to cut the shapes out of construction paper.

3. Review Chapter 3, beginning on page 15, and build your own design based on the steps listed in that chapter.

If you are stumped and cannot seem to get a design to come together with the design elements provided, take a break and look in some other areas for inspiration.

Access the Internet and type "art deco" into your favorite search engine. You will be amazed at the number of websites available for research. Look for sites devoted to architecture, furniture, ceramics, and jewelry, for starters.

Another possibility would be a trip to your local library. Look at books devoted to the 1920s and 1930s, as well as books devoted to art deco.

If you live in or near a community with a historical district or one with old buildings, you may very well find some architectural elements that might inspire you. Be sure to take your camera along to record your findings.

Other areas to investigate are textile, wallpaper, and rug designs. Although somewhat limited in scope, these are an excellent source of both geometric and abstract designs to work from.

Keep in mind as you do your research that most of the things that you will see, from a skyscraper to a teapot and everything in between, are made up of simple geometric shapes. Some may have been combined in unusual ways.

Many of these shapes are common to the world of quilting, and you may have used some of them in the past.

Project quilt design components

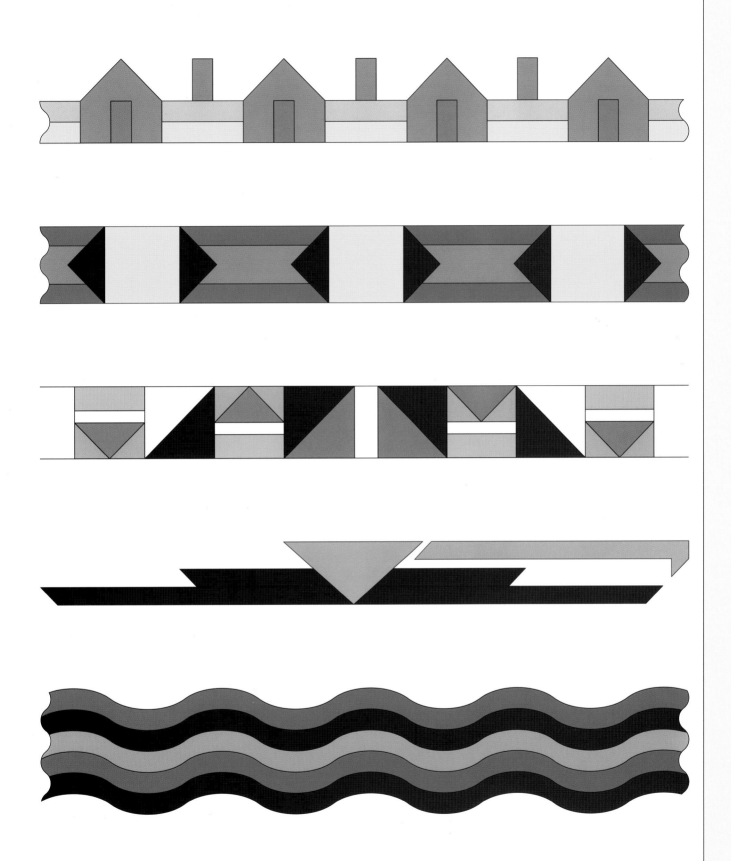

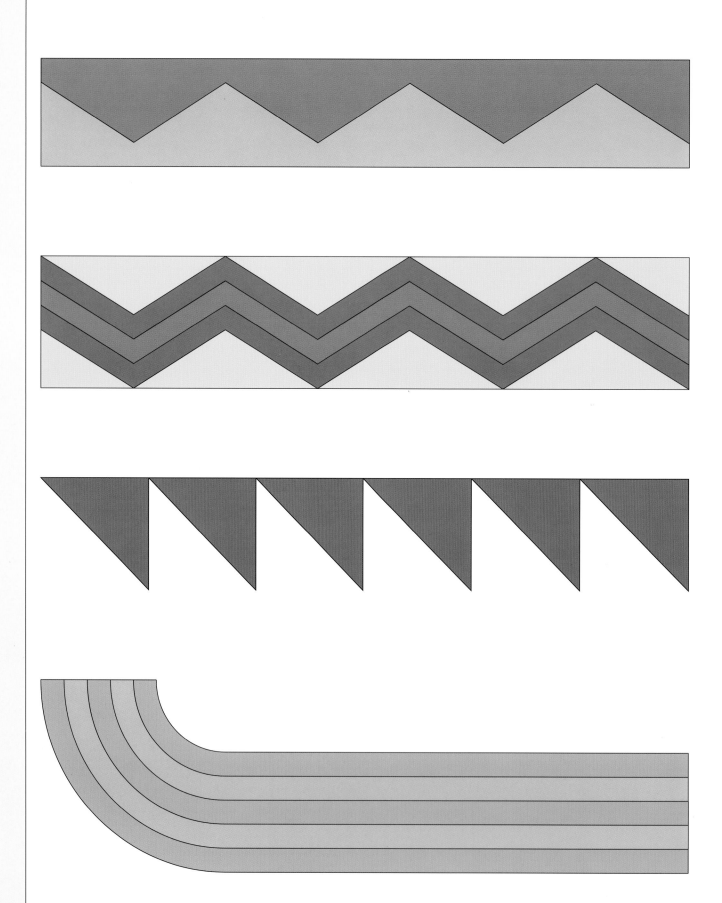

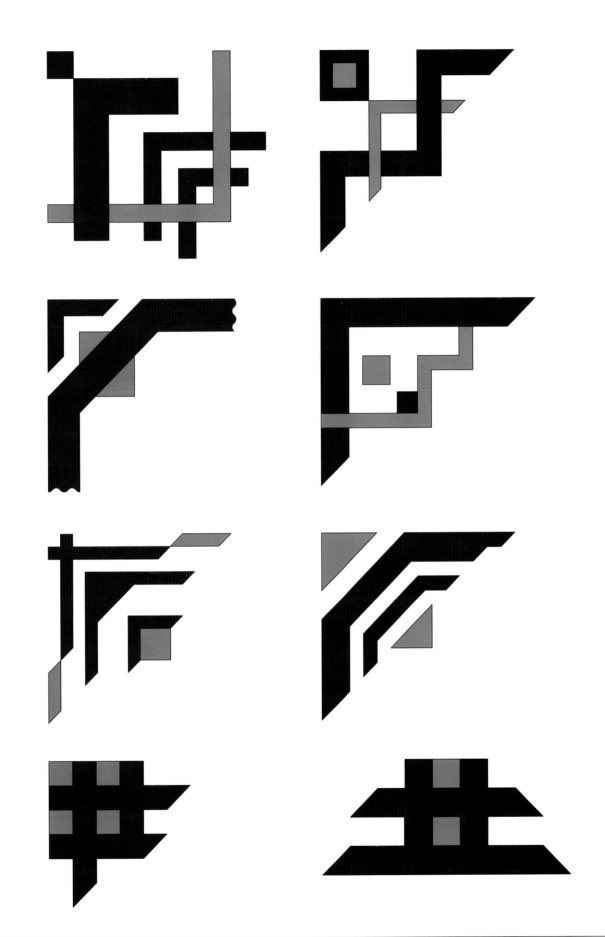

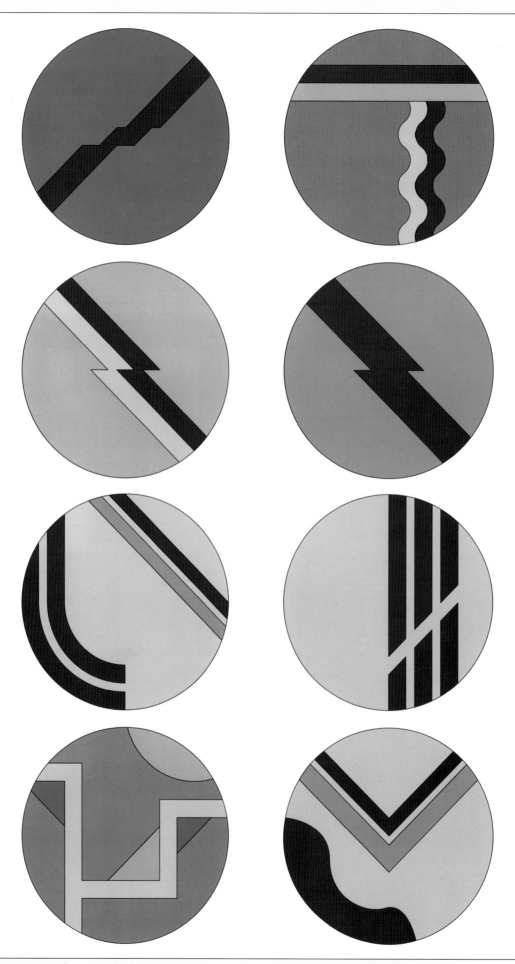

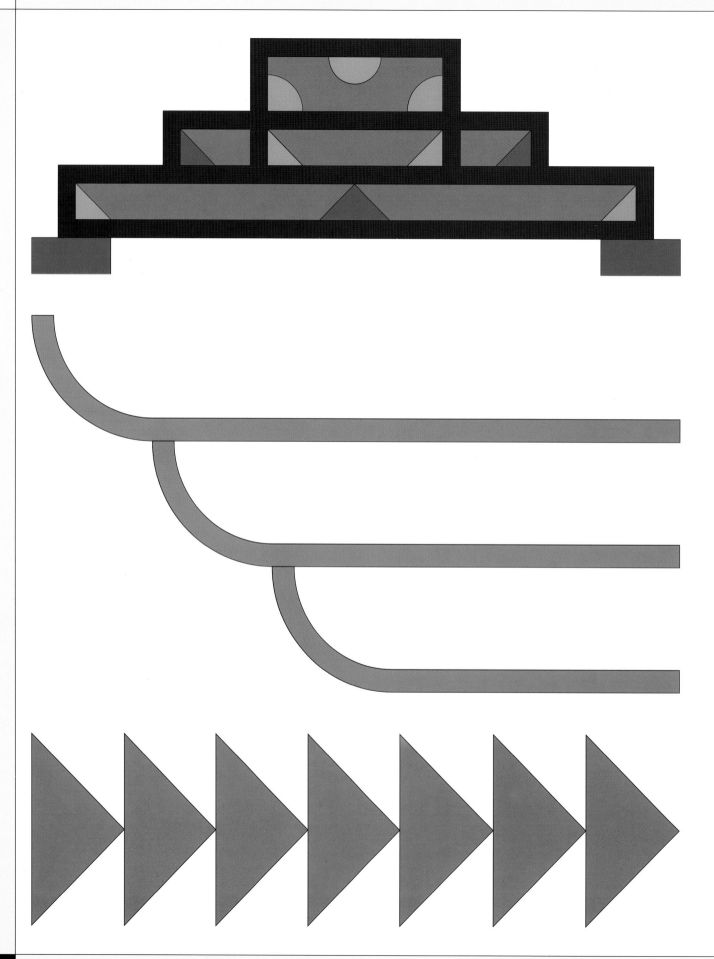

ABOUT THE AUTHOR

Don Linn lives in Redding, California, with his wife and high school sweetheart, Donna. He and Donna have a grown son and daughter who also live in California.

Since childhood, Don has loved to make things and to work with his hands. His first sewing projects involved automobile upholstery and making clothes for himself and his wife while in college.

Don had an entire career working in various manufacturing facilities as a draftsman. It was here that he dealt with a wide array of geometric shapes while doing machine design work before returning to college. After college he worked in upper management in both the forest products industry and the precast concrete industry. During this time he drew upon his experience as a draftsman in designing machinery and doing production drawings.

Don's journey in quilting began after a corporate downsizing. He started out with a longarm machine and not a clue how to operate it. Since then, he has taught himself how to machine quilt, design, and piece quilts. He is now a well-known teacher of machine quilting and piecing classes.

While doing research for quilt designs Don came across the wonderful geometric designs so prevalent in the art deco style. It was a simple transition from drafting the geometric shapes he used in his design work to incorporating those shapes in his art deco quilts, and that is how this book was born.

Don's website: www.mrquilt.com

Other books by Don Linn

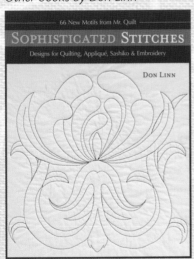

Great Titles *from* C&T PUBLISHING

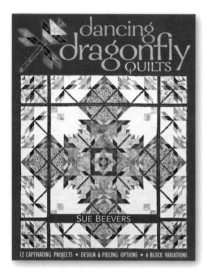

Available at your local retailer or **www.ctpub.com** *or* **800-284-1114**

For a list of other fine books from C&T Publishing, ask for a free catalog:

C&T PUBLISHING, INC.

P.O. Box 1456
Lafayette, CA 94549
800-284-1114

Email: ctinfo@ctpub.com
Website: www.ctpub.com

C&T Publishing's professional photography services are now available to the public. Visit us at www.ctmediaservices.com.

Tips and Techniques can be found at www.ctpub.com > Consumer Resources > Quiltmaking Basics: Tips & Techniques for Quiltmaking & More

For quilting supplies:

COTTON PATCH

1025 Brown Ave.
Lafayette, CA 94549
Store: 925-284-1177
Mail order: 925-283-7883

Email: CottonPa@aol.com
Website: www.quiltusa.com

Note: Fabrics used in the quilts shown may not be currently available, as fabric manufacturers keep most fabrics in print for only a short time.